The Natural Banjo Player
Nature's Lessons for Effortless Playing
By Rick McKeon

Copyright 2016 Rick McKeon

Welcome!

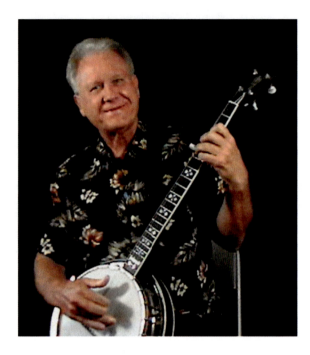

If you study nature closely you will understand the strategies and techniques that the natural world has developed over millions of years! Many of these strategies can be applied to the banjo. With practice, your banjo playing will become enjoyable, natural and effortless!

Nature flows. Wind and water move effortlessly through an environment filled with obstacles. Observing plants and animals can teach us how they accomplish amazing feats with minimal effort. You might be thinking, "I'm not a tree or drop of water. What does this have to do with me?" Well, that's what I hope to explain in this book.

I have gleaned these insights over a lifetime study of music and nature, and now I will show you how to apply them to your banjo playing.

Each chapter presents a lesson learned from nature. I have tried to maintain a consistent organization where each chapter has:

1. An Overview of the Concept.
2. An Activity where you go out in nature and make some observations.
3. An Exercise that gives you a chance to apply the concept to the banjo.

It is my hope that the concepts contained in this book will make your banjo playing more interesting and enjoyable, but it's also my desire that you will be inspired to get out and enjoy nature at a deeper level. I believe that we are meant to live in harmony with the natural world. We should feel just as much at home laying on the soft grass of a mountain meadow as we are at home sitting in our nice comfy recliner.

This is a reference book and a workbook with practical exercises to illustrate each concept. As such, you don't need to work your way from beginning to end. Feel free to jump around and spend more time on some concepts and less time on others. Many of these concepts are fun to just think about, but I also want this to be a hands-on playing book.

So, pick up your banjo and let's get started!

Table of Contents

Chapter 1. Flow Like a River — 8
1.1 Water and Wind — 8
Activity 1.1 Spend Some Time Observing Nature's Flow — 9
Exercise 1.1 Practice This Approach on the Banjo — 9
Exercise 1.2 Apply This Approach to a Familiar Song — 10

Chapter 2. Conservation of Motion — 11
2.1 Go to the Ant — 11
Activity 2.1 Discover Examples of Conservation of Motion — 13
Exercise 2.1 Stay Close to the Strings — 15
Exercise 2.2 Guide and Pivot Fingers — 16
Exercise 2.3 Right Hand Motion — 19

Chapter 3. Conservation of Energy — 21
3.1 The Beauty and Grace of a Seagull in Flight — 21
Activity 3.1 How Nature Conserves Energy — 22
Exercise 3.1 The Play and Relax Technique — 22
Exercise 3.2 Only Enough Pressure — 24
Exercise 3.3 Partial Chords and Open Strings — 24
Exercise 3.4 Apply These Techniques to a Song — 25

Chapter 4. Focus on the Target — 26
4.1 Observe the Eagle, the Fox and the Frog — 26
Activity 4.1 Watch Creatures in the Wild — 26
Exercise 4.1 Slides — 27
Exercise 4.2 Chord Planting — 27

Chapter 5. A Variety of Sounds — 28
5.1 The Sounds of Nature — 28
5.2 The Heart of Music is Timing — 29

5.3 The Soul of Music is Dynamics	30
Activity 5.1 Listen to Nature's Sounds	31
Exercise 5.1 Apply These Lessons to Your Playing	31

Chapter 6. The Natural Approach to Practice — 32

6.1 Natural Forces	32
6.2 Once I Was a Mucker	33
Activity 6.1 Learn How Nature Does It	34
Exercise 6.1 Natural Practice	35

Chapter 7. The Natural Approach to Playing — 37

7.1 Pet Your Dog	37
Activity 7.1 Understand This Approach	38
Exercise 7.1 Apply This Approach to the Banjo	38

Chapter 8. Nature Sings Without Worry — 39

8.1 Birds Don't Worry about What Others Think	39
Activity 8.1 Observe Animal Behavior	40
Exercise 8.1 Don't Worry, Be Happy!	40

Chapter 9. Anticipation Means No Surprises — 41

9.1 Bird on a Wire	41
Activity 9.1 Observe Animal and Insect Behavior	41
Exercise 9.1 Anticipate Chord Changes	42
Exercise 9.2 Slides That Put Your Left Hand in Position	43
Exercise 9.3 Right Hand Picking	43
Exercise 9.4 Read Ahead	44

Chapter 10. Strength — 45

10.1 The Bear	45
10.2 Strength Makes It a Lot Easier	45
Activity 10.1 Observe Nature and Observe Great Players	46
Exercise 10.1 Strength in Your Hands	46

Chapter 11. Momentum — 47
11.1 Momentum in Natural Events — 47
Activity 11.1 Look for Examples of Momentum — 48
Exercise 11.1 Use Past Successes to Move You Forward — 48

Chapter 12. Nature's Balance — 49
12.1 The Balancing Act — 49
12.2 Predictability and Surprise — 50
12.3 Tension and Release — 52
12.4 Anticipation and Fulfillment — 53
12.5 Repetition with Variations — 54
12.6 Tempo and Dynamics — 55
12.7 Attraction toward a Tonal Center — 57
Activity 12.1 Study Nature's Balance — 58
Exercise 12.1 Apply These Lessons to Your Banjo Playing — 58

Chapter 13. Limitations and Setbacks — 59
13.1 Nature Thrives Despite Limitations — 59
13.2 The Ant in the Parking Lot — 61
13.3 The Principle of Renewal — 61
Activity 13.1 Look for Examples of Persistence Despite Limitations — 62
Exercise 13.1 Let's Get Specific — 62

Chapter 14. Knowledge — 64
14.1 Humans vs. Stronger Animals — 64
Activity 14.1 Make a Plan to Increase Your Musical Knowledge — 65
Exercise 14.1 Use Knowledge to Improve Your Playing — 66

Chapter 15. Nature's Diversity — 67
15.1 Nature's Diverse Community — 67
Activity 15.1 Observe Unique Strengths — 68
Exercise 15.1 Decisions Based on Your Unique Strengths — 69

Chapter 16. Nature's Jam session — 70

16.1 Balance, Harmony and Interaction — 70
16.2 Mountain Music — 71
16.3 Trees and Rocks — 72
Activity 16.1 Take Time to Just Listen — 73
Exercise 16.1 Record Some Interesting Sounds — 74
Exercise 16.2 Let's Jam! — 74

Chapter 17. Where Do We Go from Here? — 75

17.1 The Adventure Continues — 75

Meet the Author — 76

Other Books by Rick McKeon — 77

Chapter 1. Flow Like a River

Figure 1.1: Flow Like a River

1.1 Water and Wind

Nature has a balance and flow that we can learn from. Think about water and wind. Think about nature's cycles both short and long, and let your banjo playing become fluid.

This first lesson is about fluid motion and how to allow your left hand to move over the fingerboard like water flowing in a stream. What a lovely and natural concept! After all, we are playing music. Shouldn't the mechanics of right and left hand be smooth and fluid?

Activity 1.1 Spend Some Time Observing Nature's Flow

To understand this concept we need to spend some time observing nature's flow. This is important. Don't just think about it, go out and do this activity. Even if you have spent a lot of time in nature, do this again.

Find a nice quiet spot by a stream where you can sit comfortably for a while. Don't be in a hurry - take plenty of time to relax, to listen, and to watch the motion of the water. Observe how the water finds its way effortlessly around obstacles. What does it sound like? Do you hear higher and lower pitched sounds? Is there a little waterfall where bubbles are formed? Become familiar with this stream. Get to know it as best you can.

Now, picture the banjo fingerboard and your left hand moving over it like the water in this stream. Imagine fretting notes and forming chords with this same smooth flow between them. For the motion of your left hand to be smooth you have to know where you are going ahead of time. So think of moving smoothly between specific chords or fretting specific notes.

This should be a relaxing and enjoyable experience. Don't struggle with it or get frustrated. We're starting to build the habit of "relaxed concentration."

If there isn't a stream close by, you can accomplish the same thing by observing the wind blowing through the trees, ocean waves lapping the shore, or any similar natural flowing motion.

Exercise 1.1 Practice This Approach on the Banjo

Let's practice this motion on the banjo.

We're going to strum I, IV, V, I (G, C, D, G) with a nice slow flowing motion of the left hand as we move between chords. Forget the 5th string for now. Just strum the first four strings. Strum each chord twice and then move to the next one. As you practice this exercise think back to your experience observing the flowing stream, and make your left hand imitate the water.

Figure 1.2 shows the chord forms to make:

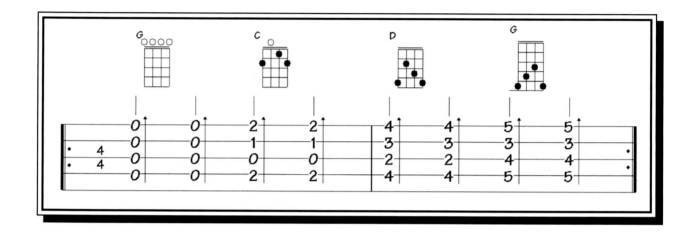

Figure 1.2: Strum I, IV, V, I

Exercise 1.2 Apply This Approach to a Familiar Song

Now, here's the fun part! Take a familiar song (make it an easy one that you know pretty well) and apply this same left hand technique to it. For it to feel natural you may have to slow it way down at first. Speed will come later. The eventual goal is to have a relaxed, flowing left hand for all of your playing.

Chapter 2. Conservation of Motion

Figure 2.1 Conservation of Motion

2.1 Go to the Ant

Over millions of years nature has designed ways to accomplish more with less effort. This means nature has developed efficiencies in terms of conservation of motion and conservation of energy. These lessons are obvious once we know how to look for them.

Have you ever wondered why anthills take on a conical form? I have watched ants carrying grains of sand from underground. They carry it right to the rim of the cone and drop it. They don't drop it before they reach the rim because it might roll back, and they don't carry it all the way down the other side – that would be a waste of energy. If they do this randomly, in all directions, a cone results.

Up here in Prescott, Arizona there was a lot of mining activity during the early 1900's. In the Bradshaw Mountains you will see lots of mines and test holes. Usually a test hole will have a conical shape just like an anthill. The old miners were doing the same thing as the ants. They had to remove some material, but they weren't going to carry it further than necessary. Near a mine shaft you will usually see a "tailings pile." Again, it is not far from the mine entrance.

Figure 2.2 below shows a miner's test hole.

Figure 2.2 Miner's Test Hole

Even nonliving things seem to conserve motion. Volcanoes and meteor craters have the same conical shape as an anthill. Do they follow the same natural laws?

In nature there are many examples of conservation of motion. Figure 2.3 below illustrates that even the vanes in a leaf have an efficient way to distribute nutrients. It's interesting to note the similarity of this picture to an aerial photograph of a residential suburb. Maybe the city planners have discovered something about efficient land use (or maximizing profit).

Figure 2.3 Vanes in a Leaf

Activity 2.1 Discover Examples of Conservation of Motion

Take a hike in the woods or visit your favorite natural place. It doesn't have to be a beautiful pine forest. You can learn these lessons at the seaside, in the desert, or even in your local city park.

Look for various examples of conservation of motion. You may come across a game trail going up over a hill. Stop and study it for a while. Would you have taken a different route or is this one pretty much the best way up over the hill?

Figure 2.4 Game Trail

Study the path a stream has taken down into a valley. Has it chosen the most efficient path? Some of these things may seem obvious, but the longer you study them the more you will learn.

I took the photo for Figure 2.5 while hiking a beautiful trail along Miller Creek in Prescott, Arizona. This creek winds its way down the hillside and through Thumb Butte Park. It's interesting that both the hiking trail and Thumb Butte Road follow the path that the stream has taken. It's a scenic and efficient way up the valley.

Figure 2.5 Miller Creek

Can you apply the concept of conservation of motion to make your banjo playing more effective and enjoyable? Let's try a few examples.

Exercise 2.1 Stay Close to the Strings

The further you move your fingers away from the strings, the further they have to come back. This applies to both the right hand and the left. This isn't rocket science, but so many times we just don't think about it.

In this exercise we are going to move between chord forms and see if we can keep our left hand fingers within one-quarter inch of the strings. Figure 2.6 below shows the chords to make. We'll start with the three basic open chords and then see if we can do the same thing fretting 4-string closed chords. As we did in Exercise 1.1, we want to keep the left hand motion fluid, but now we also want to concentrate on keeping the fingers close to the strings. Strum each chord twice and then move to the next one. Once these moves feel comfortable make sure you play them in time using a metronome.

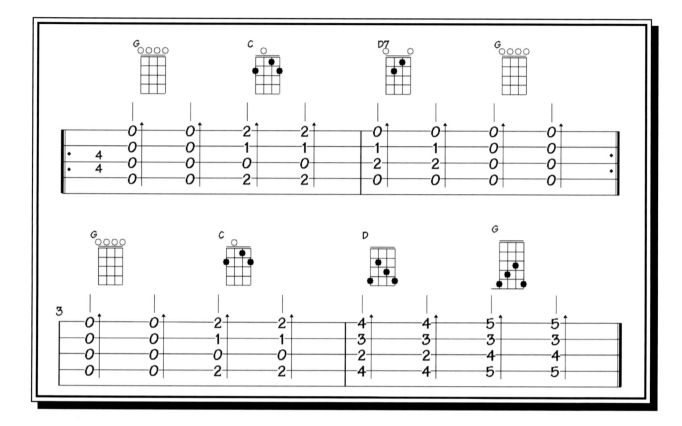

Figure 2.6 Keep Your Fingers Close to the Strings

Exercise 2.2 Guide and Pivot Fingers

Another way to reduce motion and make a smooth and efficient transition between chords is to use Guide Fingers and Pivot Fingers.

A "Guide Finger" guides your hand to the next chord. That finger frets the same string in the next chord but you have to move your left hand up or down the neck. Once you are in the new position all you have to do is put the other fretting fingers down. Because the Guide Finger stays on the same string during the transition, it guarantees economy of motion.

A "Pivot Finger" is one that stays in exactly the same place as you change from one chord to the next. Your left hand doesn't move up or down the neck. You simply place the other fingers in new positions.

Both of these techniques not only promote conservation of motion; they also help your left hand to be more stable and accurate!

Here's an easy one using your left hand index finger as a pivot finger. Change from an open C chord to a D7 and then back again keeping the index finger on the second string, 1st fret. Do this a few times and then play C, D7, Dsus, and G. Figure 2.7 shows the chord forms:

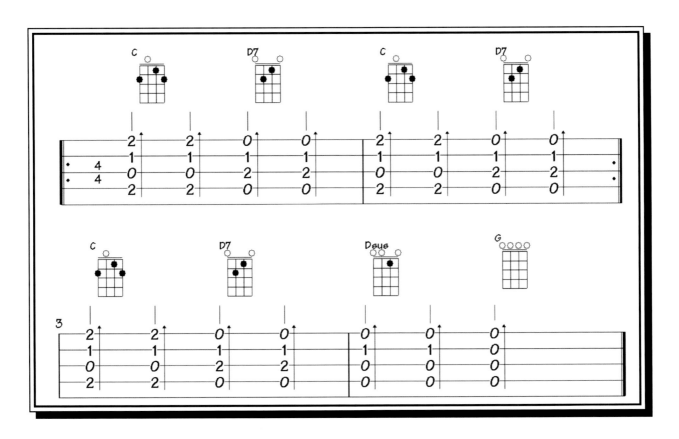

Figure 2.7 Pivot Fingers

When playing, do you typically make this change using the index finger as a pivot finger? How does it feel in your left hand? It should feel pretty natural. Notice that your hand doesn't move at all - you are just pivoting some fingers around that second string, 1st fret position.

Spend some time just messing around looking for other examples of pivot fingers. Once you find them, see if you can integrate them into your songs.

Figure 2.8 shows a simple example of using a Guide Finger (and it's also a great exercise for moving between closed position chords). In this exercise we are going to move between the G chord and D chord. Imagine your ring finger guiding your hand between these two positions. It's OK to lift the ring finger a little bit, but not much. Also, concentrate on eliminating any "scratchy" sounds as your hand moves. At first just strum and then try a little picking pattern as shown in the tab or just make up some patterns of your own.

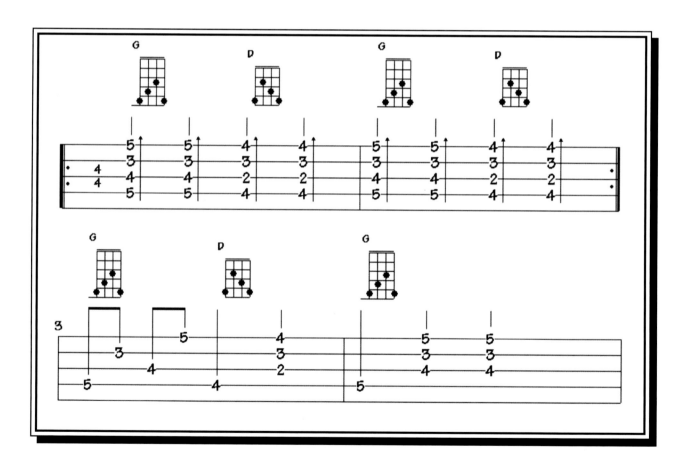

Figure 2.8 Guide Fingers

Exercise 2.3 Right Hand Motion

Conservation of motion is important for the right hand too. If you watch great banjo players it looks like their right hand isn't even moving! Now, that's conservation of motion. Real fast picking requires finger picks to reduce the drag of flesh on strings and also keeping your fingers close to the strings. Excess motion will slow you down.

Again, the question is, why let your fingers fly all over the place? You just have to come back and strike the string again. Planting a finger(s) on the head helps to keep your right hand in place.

"Anchor" is probably not the best term to use because it implies the finger is stuck to one spot really solid and can't move. A light touch is plenty for stability, and your right hand is still free to move closer to the bridge or fingerboard to achieve the dynamics and overtone content you want.

Let's practice the roll patterns shown in Figure 2.9 with minimum right hand motion. As you play these rolls keep the following in mind:

1. Keep your right hand as relaxed as possible. Try to eliminate any tension. Relaxed concentration provides for speed, strength and control.
2. Keep your right hand fingers close to the strings. Experiment a little and find the right amount of movement for efficiency and a good tone.

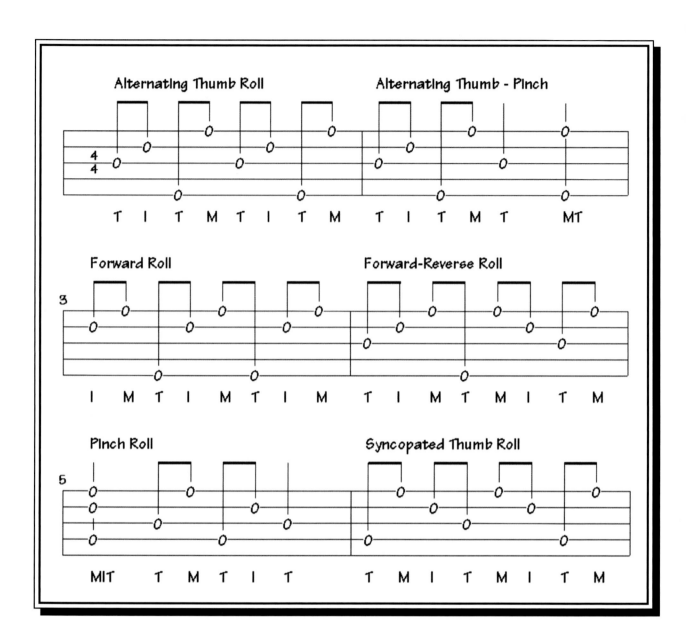

Figure 2.9 Basic Banjo Rolls

Chapter 3. Conservation of Energy

Figure 3.1 Conservation of Energy

3.1 The Beauty and Grace of a Seagull in Flight

Whenever I watch seagulls in flight I am amazed at their beauty and grace. It's as if they were made to live in the sky!

What makes for this grace? I think it's their efficiency in flight. They have to flap their wings once in a while, but they can glide through the air effortlessly. Many birds know how to catch a thermal updraft and ride it hundreds of feet. They are using the forces of nature to their advantage.

Now, humans are too heavy to fly under their own power (especially me) but we can learn a lot from the seagull.

Activity 3.1 How Nature Conserves Energy

Birds are graceful in flight, but many animals move with grace and beauty. Even trees can move gracefully in the wind. In this activity we are going to observe how plants and animals get things done with a minimum of effort.

Spend some time watching a deer as it browses or a young shoot as it breaks up through the ground. I have seen mushrooms push up heavy clods of dirt seemingly without effort.

Exercise 3.1 The Play and Relax Technique

There are many ways the conservation of energy principle can be applied to the banjo. Certainly there are times when you have to fret the strings, bend a note, make a hammer or a long reach. Sometimes we have to fret several strings at once or hold an awkward position,

BUT NOT ALWAYS!

Are you tensed up and have a "death grip" on the banjo neck all the time? If you are, you are exerting energy when you don't have to. When moving between notes or chord positions, what is your left hand doing? It should be relaxing. Even if only for a short time it should be "on vacation." The concept we are talking about here is often called, "Play and Relax."

Let's try a couple of exercises to test out this technique.

The first one involves "boom chick" vamping. You are going to be holding a 4-string G chord. When you strike the 4th string you are holding the chord down. And when you pinch the 1st three strings you are still holding the chord, but only for an instant. So, for most of beats two and four your left hand should be resting. The chord form is shown in Figure 3.2 below.

Pay special attention to your left hand on beats two and four. Is it completely relaxed or are you still feeling some tension?

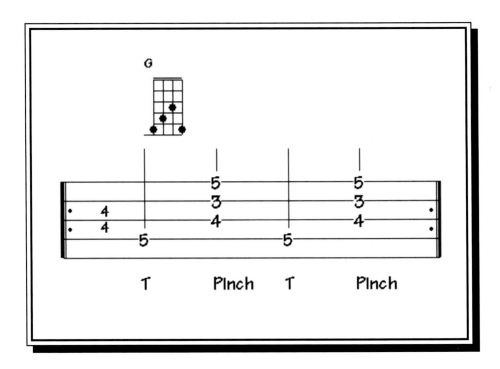

Figure 3.2 Vamping

Now, let's try an exercise where we relax the left hand while moving to a new chord position. As shown in Figure 3.3 below, we are going to play the C chord in three different forms: the open C, the C barred at the 5th fret, and the F form C at the 8th fret. Start really slow with this exercise. Pinch the 4th, 2nd and 1st strings. Pay attention to the feeling in your left hand as you move to the next position. It should be perfectly relaxed and starting to form the next chord. Once this exercise feels comfortable at a slow speed pick up the tempo.

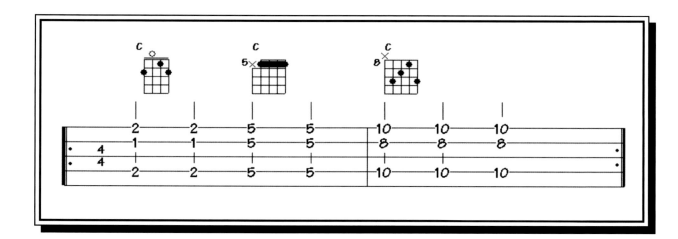

Figure 3.3 Play and Relax

Exercise 3.2 Only Enough Pressure

Another way to conserve energy when fretting single notes or chords is to use only enough pressure to get a clean sound. If you squeeze the neck too hard you will tire your left hand quickly and you can actually bend notes off pitch.

Fret a single note or chord and listen to the sound. Of course, if the sound is not good because of buzzing or muting you need to fix that. Once you are getting a good tone, try relaxing your grip a little. If the sound is still good, relax your left hand a little more. Eventually you won't be fretting hard enough to get a nice clean sound. Experiment until you are getting clean sounding notes with minimum pressure.

Exercise 3.3 Partial Chords and Open Strings

Many times we have to make full 4-string chords, but often we play only partial chords. For most songs the tablature will list a chord for a certain measure but you won't be holding that chord at all. That's because we are playing melody notes and rolls.

For this exercise look at the arrangement for one of your favorite songs and see how many times partial chords are used. Also, try to see if you can substitute a partial chord where a full chord is called for. A good example would be to substitute a 3-string D chord for the full D chord as shown in Figure 3.4 below. It often works because the open 4th string is a D note.

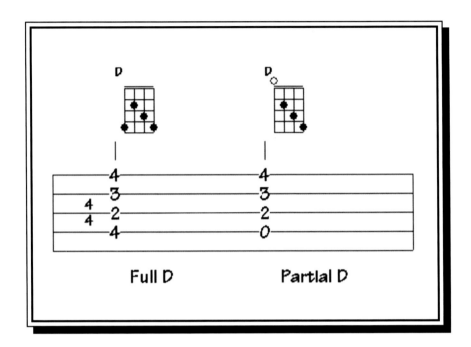

Figure 3.4 Partial Chords

Exercise 3.4 Apply These Techniques to a Song.

In these first three chapters we have talked about fluid motion, conservation of motion, and conservation of energy. Take a familiar song and see how many of these techniques you can apply to it.

Chapter 4. Focus on the Target

Figure 4.1 Focus on the Target

4.1 Observe the Eagle, the Fox and the Frog

If you have ever seen an eagle snatch a fish from a lake or a frog catch an insect you know they are focused on their target. A fox will hunt in deep snow where he can't even see the rodent he is after. He has to listen and determine where his prey will be by the time he plunges into the snow.

Activity 4.1 Watch Creatures in the Wild

Take some time to watch animals as they hunt. Notice how intently they are focused on their target. Even your pet cat can teach you lessons about concentration. Can these lessons be applied to the banjo?

Exercise 4.1 Slides

Let's consider executing a slide. For a slide to be effective we need to hear the note that we are sliding to. This means keeping your finger tight against the fingerboard, but even more importantly it means focusing on the target location. Think of concentrating the energy in the string to that spot - that's your target. Try fretting the first string at the 2nd fret, striking the string, and then sliding to the 5th fret. Don't follow your finger as it slides. Focus on the 5th fret and imagine concentrating the energy in the string to that fret. The resulting note should sound out nice and loud. After all, you are taking the energy in the string and concentrating it to a shorter string.

Just to bring this point home, wait for a while after striking the string and then do the slide. You should have complete control over the sound.

Artists use this same technique. If an artist wants to draw a line between point A and point B, he doesn't watch his hand as he draws. He focuses on the target - point B.

Exercise 4.2 Chord Planting

The same technique applies if you have to make a quick chord change. You need to know ahead of time what the chord form looks like and where it is. Then you concentrate on the target position. Try this method while moving back and forth between chords. Picture the chord first and where it is on the fingerboard, and then move your left hand.

A good practice technique when learning a new song is to simply learn the shape and position of all of the chords. Practice quickly and accurately moving through the chord progression before you start working on the actual arrangement.

Chapter 5. A Variety of Sounds

Figure 5.1 A Variety of Sounds

5.1 The Sounds of Nature

The natural world has an amazing variety of sounds. One of my favorite things to do when out in the woods is to just stop and listen. At first I hear the obvious things like the wind blowing through the trees, the sound of a nearby stream and birds singing. Then I start to hear more subtle sounds like insects buzzing or leaves falling to the ground.

But there is more than just the sounds themselves. Each sound has its own variations, rhythms and dynamics. The wind doesn't just blow. It can blow faster or slower, louder or softer, and it has intermittent gusts. The stream has little waterfalls with different rhythms and frequencies. What an amazing symphony!

Birds have conversations. Sometimes it may be a mating call and other times it might be a warning. The other day while I was out on a hike a squirrel started chattering like crazy. I finally realized he was chattering at me! If we become attuned to the sounds of nature we can learn many lessons about rhythm, dynamics and sound production. The sounds we produce on the banjo are basically that of a vibrating string, but we also produce percussive sounds, notes with various mixtures of harmonic content, and notes with a broad dynamic range. The banjo can sound like a restful sunset or a gathering storm.

5.2 The Heart of Music is Timing

Figure 5.2 Nature's Rhythms

One of the most common issues for beginning banjo players is the lack of solid timing. Typically they will play the easier parts faster and the harder parts slower. Also, things may go along pretty well until there is a chord change. Sound familiar?

If your timing is rock solid your playing will sound musical. But if your timing is not solid it will never sound like music. You may play all of the right notes and play them fast, but it won't be music.

Nature is filled with rhythms, from waves lapping on the shore of a lake to crickets chirping. Becoming familiar with nature's rhythms will help us develop an "internal clock" that will influence our playing. Being aware of rhythm and listening for it everywhere will carry over to our playing.

5.3 The Soul of Music is Dynamics

Figure 5.3 Gathering Storm

To be interesting music must have dynamics. I'm using this term in a broad sense to include loud and soft, but also to include accent, staccato and legato, bright and mellow, and variations in tempo. These things make music expressive and moving. The sounds of nature contain all of these elements. We just have to stop and listen.

Activity 5.1 Listen to Nature's Sounds

Spend as much time as you can listening to nature's rhythms, dynamics and variations. Can you start to hear intricate patterns? Listen to wind, water, birdsong, and even the beating of your own heart.

A gust of wind can teach us about dynamics, and the sound of a woodpecker can teach us about staccato.

Exercise 5.1 Apply These Lessons to Your Playing

While you are out in nature take note of any musical insights you may have. When you get home see if you can apply them to your banjo.

Analyze a familiar tune that you have played for years an experiment with the lessons you have brought home from the forest or seaside. Have fun and experiment! Here are some suggestions:

1. Choose specific measures that you want to play louder or softer.
2. Find a place in the song for a crescendo or "lightning strike."
3. Alternate between bright and mellow sounds by moving your right hand closer to the bridge or closer to the fingerboard.
4. Make the entire piece sound like a summer day or a sparkling stream.
5. For a quiet piece, picture a sunset as you play.
6. Use a tempo change to picture an impending storm.
7. The options are limitless!

Chapter 6. The Natural Approach to Practice

Figure 6.1 Go with the Flow

6.1 Natural Forces

When we start to understand a rushing stream or a powerful wind we recognize that we cannot fight these forces. We will lose every time! The lesson here is don't "struggle" with your banjo practice. Learn to "go with the flow" and direct those forces yourself.

Watching a bird glide and soar on the wind gives us a perfect example. Instead of fighting the wind, they use it to get where they want to go.

Sailors have learned the same lesson. A sailboat can go to a place that is upwind by tacking back and forth at an angle. If you study a game trail or hiking trail going up the side of a hill you will see the advantage of taking switchbacks instead of trying to go straight up the side. That approach is more pleasurable and less dangerous.

When I say, "go with the flow" I don't mean to be lazy or to not exert any effort. What I mean is to take an intelligent and natural approach to your practice and playing. Don't tough it out for hours. Don't hurt yourself. Make your practice sessions shorter and more frequent. Don't hold chord positions until you hurt your hand. Take a break and enjoy what you have accomplished.

Be involved emotionally as well as physically. Learning takes place more quickly if there is a positive emotional state involved. So, be involved and take pleasure in small accomplishments.

Think about the saying, "light is right." Fingerpicks reduce the drag of flesh against strings and promote speed. A light touch while fretting promotes beautiful sound, quicker chord changes, and doesn't tire your left hand.

6.2 Once I was a Mucker

Without getting into all the technical details of copper mining, just let me say that copper can be leached out of the ore with acid. Once in solution it can be precipitated out on tin cans. So how do you wash the copper mud off the tin cans? Enter the mucker!

These tin cans with copper mud all over them are stacked in a chamber with a wire mesh floor. The mucker uses a high-pressure hose to wash off the mud. When I say "high pressure" I mean really high pressure! The first time I was down in that chamber the fire hose threw me from one side to the other. The pressure was stronger than I was. With a little experience and some training I learned to brace the hose against a wall and let the wall take the pressure. Then all I had to do was direct the water where I wanted it to go. Easy! The idea was that instead of fighting it I was merely directing these strong forces. If you have ever tried to run a commercial floor buffer you have had a similar experience.

Activity 6.1 Learn How Nature Does It

Nature's forces can be powerful and environments can be hostile, but plants and animals have found ways to deal with these forces. Go out for a hike or take a trip to the park and look for clues. Study plants and animals as they thrive in hostile environments. Watch birds circle and effortlessly ride the wind. Observe how fish swim in a flowing stream or how a mushroom breaks through the ground.

Figure 6.2 Mushroom Pushing up through the Ground

Exercise 6.1 Natural Practice

How can we apply this lesson to our banjo practice? If we take a more natural, thoughtful, and less strained approach to practice we will make faster progress and enjoy it a lot more along the way!

Several short practice sessions are more productive than one marathon session. Your learning will be quicker and you won't risk hurting your hands.

Another way to not fight against external forces that may distract you is to eliminate them. Have a practice environment that is an enjoyable place to be and doesn't have lots of distractions. This way you won't be trying to "swim upstream." You will be giving yourself every advantage possible.

Be present and involved both mentally and emotionally as you practice. I am not a big proponent of unconscious practice while watching TV. There was a popular movement back in the 70's regarding "sleep learning." The idea was that you could play a tape while you were asleep and learn. I was teaching high school during that time and found that those students who were actively involved in class did a lot better on tests than those who fell asleep in class.

Another way to go with the flow and not fight it is to make sure your banjo is set up for ease of playing. If the action is too high you will be struggling to fret notes and make chords. Some banjos are easier to play than others, but you should have your banjo set up as good as it can be.

There's nothing wrong with just having fun noodeling around on the banjo. It can be a lot of fun, and you may discover some nice licks or an interesting chord progression. But the most effective way to practice technique or to learn a new song is to have a specific goal for the practice session. You should be able to state this goal in one sentence. It should be specific, realistic and measurable. In this way you are directing your time and energy instead of being pulled every which way.

If you make a breakthrough or have a pleasant experience during practice, make the most of it. Take pleasure in it and use it to propel you forward. You will be like that bird catching a thermal.

Chapter 7. The Natural Approach to Playing

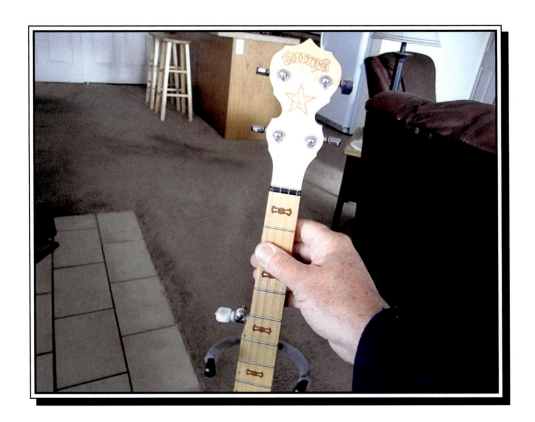

Figure 7.1 Reach for Your Banjo

7.1 Pet Your Dog

When you reach for your banjo what are you thinking? What are you feeling? Do you feel tension or nervousness? Are you hoping maybe you'll do better today than you did yesterday? Or is it like reaching out to an old friend, or maybe reaching out to pet your dog?

There is a huge difference between these two approaches. If it is all about right and wrong and avoiding mistakes, it's not going to be a pleasurable practice session. If you reach for your banjo like you are reaching out to pet your dog it will be a pleasurable and productive session! Have you been waiting all day until you finally get home and can play your banjo or are you practicing because you know you should? Is waiting to play your banjo like waiting for the pizza to arrive? If so, you're on the right track. It's all in the approach. After all, why are you playing the banjo in the first place?

Activity 7.1 Understand This Approach

This is a simple yet powerful concept. Your pleasure and your progress depend on the approach you take. I have taught many banjo students and can pretty much tell when they are getting ready to quit. There's nothing wrong with taking a break from banjo playing for a while, but if it gets to the point where you are not having fun, you will quit for good.

Most of us are not professional musicians and don't intend to be. We don't depend on banjo playing for our living. We just like the sound and enjoy making music. Of course we want to improve, but if it becomes all about perfection instead of progress, we are in trouble.

It's good to think back on why you wanted to play the banjo in the first place. Keep it light and fun and simple. When you reach out for your banjo do it as if you were reaching out to pet your dog.

Exercise 7.1 Apply This Approach to the Banjo

This is a pretty simple assignment. As you are getting ready to practice or play, take a moment to visualize yourself enjoying it. Don't think about the bad habits you are trying to overcome or the difficult passage you are going to be working on. Just get ready to enjoy playing the banjo again!

Chapter 8. Nature Sings Without Worry

Figure 8.1 Sing with Confidence

8.1 Birds Don't Worry about What Others Think!

The picture of this Yellow Warbler inspires me!

I'm one of those people who has been insecure all of my life. I'm always looking for approval and worried that I might not get it. This insecurity has held me back on so many occasions! I'm talking about important business decisions and career advancement too. It may come from my childhood - who knows? The important thing is that we (you and me) need to get over insecurities and dump the ego related fear. We need to just enjoy playing the banjo without being timid and scared.

This concept hit me last summer when I was out on a hike. A little bird started singing a lovely song. He didn't look around to see what the other birds thought of his song. He couldn't care less! He sang with confidence and joy. This is just what he does - he sings!

I have worked with many students who were timid players. They played very quietly with a timid approach. When I told them to dig in and play with strength and confidence they said they were afraid of making mistakes. My reply of course was, "If you make a mistake we want to hear it. Then we can work with it." I also tell them that they <u>will</u> make mistakes and add, "I am going to ask you to do stuff you've never done before. Of course you will make mistakes. I make mistakes all the time." I am quick to add, "These lessons are a place to experiment, try new things, and make mistakes. That's what learning is all about."

Tension and worry can destroy your playing. If you are relaxed and enjoying your banjo playing others will enjoy it too - even if you make mistakes. Take your cue from that little bird and concentrate more on the joy of playing and less on making mistakes.

Activity 8.1 Observe Animal Behavior

Go out in the woods and learn a lesson from nature. Find a nice relaxing spot and spend a while listening to how the birds, insects and animals sing their songs. We as humans can be too reserved and worried about perfection. Bring home their attitude. Your banjo playing may not be perfect right now, but it will get better. This is a life long journey. Just enjoy the trip!

Exercise 8.1 Don't Worry, Be Happy!

I don't mean to oversimplify things by saying "Don't worry, be happy" but it is just about that simple. And there is more to it than that. For your banjo playing to sound good you have to play with strength and confidence. It really does make a difference in the sound you produce. So, take a lesson from that little bird and sing with confidence and joy!

Chapter 9. Anticipation Means No Surprises

Figure 9.1 No Surprises

9.1 Bird on a Wire

The picture above is of an Osprey landing on its nest. When you see a bird landing in a tree or on a telephone wire you are witnessing an amazing feat of flying. Unless it's a Gooney Bird, the landing will probably be perfect. It knows exactly where it wants to land and how to perform the maneuver. There are no surprises here. It doesn't have to wonder, "What should I do next?" This same principle of anticipating an event for perfect execution also applies to our banjo playing.

Activity 9.1 Observe Animal and Insect Behavior

Take a field trip out into the wild and look for examples of anticipation. Don't just take note of them, but study them in as much detail as you can. If you are watching a bird land in a tree, try to put yourself in its place. How do you slow down for the landing? Do you reach out with your feet ahead of you? How do you avoid hitting a branch?

Look for other examples. Even trees will anticipate the arrival of spring by sprouting out new growth. Sometimes they can be caught off guard by a late freeze, but usually they are good predictors of the change of season. Ants and bears know when to prepare for hibernation. Many of nature's lessons regarding anticipation can be applied to the banjo.

Figure 9.2 New Growth

Exercise 9.1 Anticipate Chord Changes

Every song has a chord progression associated with it. Once you know the song you can hear the changes coming up and be ready for them. So many times beginning banjo players are so focused on playing the current measure correctly that they are caught by surprise when the chord changes. If you are thinking ahead (or reading ahead if using tab) then you will be ready for the change, and not be caught off guard.

A good practice for anticipating chord changes is to listen to recordings or attend jam sessions and just listen. At first you may hear a change coming up, but don't know which chord it is going to be. With practice you will anticipate the change and know (usually) what chord it is.

Most simple 3-chord songs use the I, IV and V chords. Another good practice is to just pick a familiar song and strum along as you sing it. If you hear a change coming up you only have two choices because you are already playing one of the three chords. So, when the change comes just pick a chord. You will know soon enough if you picked the right one. Again, with practice you will start picking the correct chord more often.

Exercise 9.2 Slides That Put Your Left Hand in Position

When you perform a slide, which finger do you slide with? Anticipating what comes next in the song and where you want your left hand to end up helps you to determine what finger to use for the slide. Your choice of slide finger can make it awkward or easy to fret the next note of the song. Anticipation makes for smooth and accurate playing.

Look at the songs you currently play with an eye to slide finger. In each case ask yourself, "Can there be a better choice?"

Exercise 9.3 Right Hand Picking

With experience, choosing which right hand finger to pluck a string with becomes fairly natural, but at first we may have to make some conscious choices. Anticipating what comes next will influence those choices.

For the common G-lick shown in Figure 9.3 below which finger is the best choice for striking the 3rd string on the "and" of beat two?

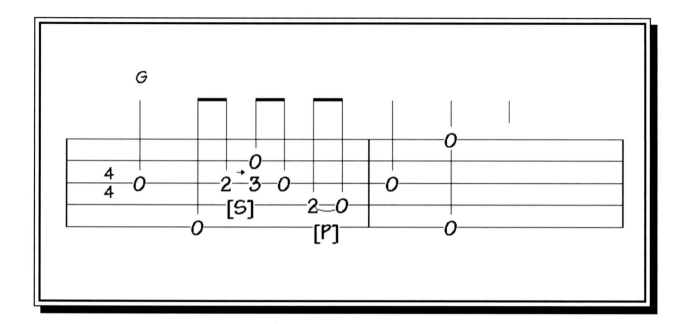

Figure 9.3 G Lick

I would choose the Index finger followed by the Middle finger on the open second string at the top of the slide. After that, the Index finger again on the "and " of beat three. Try those choices and see if you agree. Again, we're anticipating what comes next in the song.

Exercise 9.4 Read Ahead

This lesson may seem obvious but based on lots of experience with students, it isn't always obvious. When using tablature as a learning aid one of the best ways to anticipate what comes next is to read ahead.

Once you have seen the tab for the measure you are currently playing, look ahead at the next measure or two. I will often tell a student, "While you are playing this G measure be thinking D7." And of course they are not just thinking D7, they are planning ahead for the move to the new position.

Chapter 10. Strength

Figure 10.1 Strength

10.1 The Bear

The bear is a powerful animal! That strength and power come in handy. He can tear a hollow log apart to get at a beehive, and he can smash the window out of your car to get the food you (shouldn't have) left there. In nature many animals use their strength to good advantage.

10.2 Strength Makes It a Lot Easier

Strength in your right and left hands makes banjo playing easier too. Many techniques become easier and more musical with strength. The problem for many beginning players isn't that they don't know what to do, it's because they don't have the strength to do it properly.

I have noticed that many times we would just be talking casually and holding a chord when a student would let go of the banjo and shake his hand out. I always thought that strange until I realized his left hand was hurting. Think how much easier things would be if you had the strength of a bear! We don't have the strength of a bear, but we need strength in our hands.

I used to be a sheet metal cutter. At first my right hand would hurt like crazy after only a short time. With experience, I could cut sheet metal for extended periods without any discomfort! The same concept applies to banjo playing.

Activity 10.1 Observe Nature and Observe Great Players

This book is about learning lessons from nature, but part of this activity involves observing great banjo players too. Spend some time observing powerful animals and powerful natural forces, but also spend some time watching the great banjo players. Have you ever thought that great players make it look effortless? Well, for them it is. Why? Because they have experience, but also they have strength. They have the strength to hold a slide note tightly against the fingerboard without losing volume. They have the calluses on their fingertips so fretting the strings doesn't hurt.

Exercise 10.1 Strength in Your Hands

There are spring-loaded gizmos out there that you can squeeze to strengthen your grip, and there are recommended exercise routines, but I think the best exercise for playing chords is to play chords. By holding a chord and then switching to another chord and back again you will strengthen your left hand. Not only that, if you do this in time with a metronome you will be learning how to make good sounding, accurate chords. Give it a try. Just pick a few 4-string chords and transition between them. Do this exercise very slowly at first, and then pick up the tempo as you can. Use a metronome and make it musical!

Chapter 11. Momentum

Figure 11.1 Momentum

11.1 Momentum in Natural Events

If you've ever seen a rockslide or a snow avalanche, you have seen momentum build as potential energy is converted into kinetic energy. Because of the built up momentum, the event will continue even after it has reached the bottom of the mountain.

The same is true in our personal lives. Have you ever received positive feedback for something you did? Have you ever experienced joy in your banjo playing or had that "aha" moment when things finally fell in place? These things create momentum that can move us forward.

Activity 11.1 Look for Examples of Momentum

On your next hike or camping trip be on the lookout for examples of momentum in nature. Rarely do we get to witness a rockslide or snow avalanche, but you may see water splashing up on a stream bank or a stone rolling down the side of a hill. Maybe the wind is blowing and a leaf continues to move for a ways even after the gust. You might see a bird just gliding gracefully through the air. These are examples of how momentum keeps things moving. Do any of these relate to our banjo playing?

Exercise 11.1 Use Past Successes to Move You Forward

Take some time to think back on your past successes and moments of joy. Use these to inspire you and move you forward. Apply this momentum to your banjo playing. Remember your excitement when you got your first new (OK, maybe it was used) banjo? How you couldn't wait to start playing it? Use that feeling to inspire your playing today.

Do you remember when your first song started to sound pretty good and you wanted to play it for your spouse? Use that as momentum to perfect the song you are working on now. Once you have it worked out you will experience that excitement once again!

Chapter 12. Nature's Balance

Figure 12.1 Nature's Balance

12.1 The Balancing Act

Music is a balancing act. There has to be some predictability, but not so much that it becomes repetitive and boring. Tension creates movement, but we like for that tension to eventually be resolved. If we lead the listener to anticipate something, we need to fulfill that anticipation. For music to be interesting there has to be some dynamic variation. Even if we are playing a piece of music "as written" we need to express these various elements on the banjo.

Can you see these elements in nature? I'll cite a few examples, but I bet you can find many more! Study the following series of pictures with these musical elements in mind. Don't just give them a quick glance and then go on to see what I say about them. Think about each one for a while with the concepts of balance and movement in mind. I believe each one tells a story and each one has a lesson that we can apply to our banjo playing. I have placed labels on them, but you may see something different. Probably each picture could have several different captions.

In this chapter we are going to learn nature's lessons that make music come alive on the banjo.

12.2 Predictability and Surprise

Figure 12.2 What's Around the Corner?

To feel comfortable and familiar, a piece of music needs to have some structure and predictability. It can't be just a bunch of random, unconnected notes. For most listeners that would be too chaotic and not pleasing. The listener needs to have a sense of where the music is going, and is pleased when it arrives at that destination. But if it is too predictable it gets boring really fast. I have heard many songs where they take one little theme and just "beat it to death." After a short time I'm thinking, "When are they going to get off this lick and change something?" Usually I stop listening before they do.

Figure 12.2 is a photograph I took on the trail coming down from Whitney summit to Trail Crest. The trail is clearly marked, but what's around the corner? I am comfortable because I know I'm not going to get lost, but excited to find out where it goes.

When expressing a piece of music on the banjo, you can lead the listener along by clearly expressing the theme, but a little surprise here and there can add interest and excitement. This may take the form of an unexpected chord change, a variation in the melody, or an unexpected cadence at the end. Maybe you use a plagal cadence to end a piece. The listener is expecting you to go directly to the I chord, but you take a little detour to the IV chord before ending on the tonic.

12.3 Tension and Release

Figure 12.3 Tension

I personally have a problem with the terms "consonance" and "dissonance" because people tend to think of consonance as "good" and dissonance as "bad." Nothing could be farther from the truth! Music needs some tension to keep it going. We hear a little tension and then feel satisfaction when it is resolved. A suspended chord with 4 to 3 resolution has a wonderfully pleasing sound.

Half-step harmonies can be very tense. If I were to just wail away on two notes that were a half step apart, that would not be pleasing. But if I were to play through them quickly it would be exciting and pleasing.

Figure 12.3 above shows a "balancing rock" out in the Granite Basin Recreational Area of Prescott, Arizona. To me this scene has a lot of tension. I know it will be resolved, but I can't afford to wait around several million years for that to happen. In a musical composition we shouldn't have to wait millions of years for the tension to be resolved either. You as the player need to be sensitive to the amount of tension you introduce and how long you take to resolve it.

12.4 Anticipation and Fulfillment

Figure 12.4 Anticipation

I heard a story one time about a busy young executive whose son loved to play catch. The young boy asked his dad, "Can we play catch when you get home from work today?" and the dad said, "Yes, that will be great!" So the boy was excited all day long, looking forward to playing catch with his dad. When the father got home that evening he told his son, "I know I said we would play catch, but it's been a busy day and I still have a lot of work to finish tonight. We'll play catch tomorrow night."

I think you can see where this story is going. This went on night after night and eventually the boy lost interest.

When expressing a song on the banjo we can build anticipation in the listener. Before delivering on that promise we may take a little surprise detour just to perk his ears, but we need to deliver on that anticipation before long. Otherwise he will lose interest.

Figure 12.4 above is a hiking trail in the Sierra Nevada Mountains of California. I have hiked this trail into Dusy Basin many times, and after a strenuous day of hiking, I look forward to arriving at camp!

12.5 Repetition with Variations

Figure 12.5 Repetition and Variations

Many songs use repetition with variations to grab our attention and continually heighten our expectations. Ravel's Bolero is a famous classical example. Each time the theme is repeated it is more powerful than the last! Many pop, rock and bluegrass songs use this same technique.

Figure 12.5 above shows the Kearsarge Pinnacles with one of the Kearsarge Lakes in the foreground. Is your eye lead along the pinnacles to the right and then down to the lake? This to me is a natural scene that illustrates the concept of repetition with variations that lead to a specific destination. Photographers and artists look for this type of thing - musicians too!

12.6 Tempo and Dynamics

Figure 12.6 Tempo and Dynamics

We can use variations in tempo and dynamics to build a crescendo towards an important place in a composition. The listener can sense that something is about to happen.

I was camped at Rae Lakes in the Sierra Nevada Mountains when I took the photograph for Figure 12.6. There was a storm building, and it was very exciting! I knew we would be OK because our camp was already set up. Our tents were waterproof, and our sleeping bags were warm. But there was an excitement in the air wondering what was going to happen!

Figure 12.7 Tempo and Dynamics

After a long day of hiking we arrived at Sapphire Lake. It had been an exciting and strenuous day, but now it was time to relax and enjoy the peace that was descending in the basin.

As I sat in camp I was wondering how to express this peace, quiet and joy on the banjo.

12.7 Attraction toward a Tonal Center

Figure 12.8 Attraction toward a Tonal Center

When I stand on a high mountain pass and can see the mountain ranges that stretch out for miles, I often picture them as a great piano roll that could fit in "nature's player piano." What would it sound like? Something exciting I'm sure!

Figure 12.8 was taken from Kearsarge Pass looking down on Kearsarge Lakes and Bullfrog Lake to the upper right. Every song has a key signature or tonal center. This is the "home place" or "place of rest" that the song keeps coming back to. In Figure 12.8 there is a lot going on, but I see a strong attraction to Bullfrog Lake as the tonal center. Raindrops falling in this basin may meander around, but they will eventually be drawn to Bullfrog Lake.

Activity 12.1 Study Nature's Balance

I have presented a few of my discoveries about balance in nature. Now it's your turn to go out and look for inspiring lessons that you can bring home and apply to your banjo playing. Don't rush this. Just use it as an enjoyable outing in the natural world. Go to one of your favorite natural settings, relax for a while, and then start looking for all of the elements we have discussed in this chapter.

I would love to hear about what you have found! Send me an email at rmckeon5@gmail.com

Exercise 12.1 Apply These Lessons to Your Banjo Playing

I know this is a big topic, but it's OK to experiment with just one lesson at a time. Take one of the principles you have come to understand at a deeper level and apply it to just one song. Then expand on Nature's Balancing Act as it applies to your banjo playing.

Chapter 13. Limitations and Setbacks

Figure 13.1 Sky Pilot

13.1 Nature Thrives Despite Limitations

Everywhere in nature you can see life survive and even thrive under the harshest of conditions.

A seed will germinate and thrive in the crack of a rock. No one told him he couldn't survive there, so he grows and thrives there for hundreds of years.

Figure 13.2 Nature's Persistence

The water in a stream will reach its destination. It may be trapped in a pool for a while, but then it will be on its way again.

Figure 13.3 Temporary Stop along the Way

13.2 The Ant in the Parking Lot

Progress is never linear. We always progress in fits and starts with plateaus in between. A plateau is not just a flat spot. It's a place where we consolidate our gains and prepare for the next cycle of growth.

I was watching an ant hauling a heavy load across our parking lot. It was a windy day and he kept getting blown back over and over again. I'm sure the thought of giving up or quitting never entered his mind because he simply picked up his load again and kept going. Eventually he made it to the anthill!

We can learn a lesson from that ant. The lesson is that if we have setbacks, we just pick up and start moving towards our goal again. The thought of giving up shouldn't even be an option. There is no such thing as failure. We simply haven't reached our goal yet!

13.3 The Principle of Renewal

Even after a devastating fire nature has a way of recovering. The picture for Figure 13.4 below was taken about six months after the Doce Fire in Prescott, Arizona. Already you can see new growth coming back.

In our banjo playing lives, as well as life in general, we may have stagnant periods or setbacks, but if we persist we will see new growth.

Figure 13.4 Renewal

Activity 13.1 Look for Examples of Persistence

As you are out there experiencing nature, look for examples of persistence and life thriving even under harsh conditions. When you discover an example stop for a minute and ask yourself, "Is there a lesson here that I can apply in my life? Is there something specific that relates to my banjo playing?"

Exercise 13.1 Let's Get Specific

Certainly you will find many examples of persistence and adaptation in nature. So far we have been talking in general terms, but now it's time to get specific. Do you have a specific problem or limitation with regard to your banjo playing?

Maybe you are starting to get arthritis in your hands or have been injured in an accident. These things do not have to end your banjo playing adventure. You may be able to adapt to easier chord forms or even change your style of playing.

Several of my online students from around the world have sent me emails relating that they have had severe accidents, strokes, or are undergoing chemotherapy. They haven't given up, but are using their banjo playing as a major part of their recovery. How inspiring is that!

Use the lessons you have learned about nature's resilience as a source of ideas and inspiration.

Chapter 14. Knowledge

Figure 14.1 Knowledge

14.1 Humans vs. Stronger Animals

Why are humans (at this time) the dominant species on the planet? It's not because of our superior strength or speed. It's because of our superior knowledge. We may lose this position one day because we have knowledge without wisdom, but that's a discussion for another time.

Musical knowledge will allow your playing to become more insightful and interesting. Musical knowledge will allow you to communicate with other musicians more effectively, and musical knowledge will help you learn faster with less effort.

Even among the animals, look at the advantage that knowledge provides. It's a slow process, but observed over time, you can see animal intelligence increasing. Birds and apes can use tools. Dogs can understand human language to a certain extent.

Activity 14.1 Make a Plan to Increase Your Musical Knowledge

There are many facets to musical knowledge. I'm not suggesting you go to school and get a PhD in music, but there are vast recourses on the Internet that you can tap into. Here are a few possibilities for areas of study:

1. Music Theory
2. Composition
3. Music History - the banjo has a fascinating history!
4. Great banjo players and their styles (also their colorful lives!)
5. I have written a book called "Music Theory Made Really Easy" that you might like. Visit my website at rickmckeon.com
6. Even working your way through this book will broaden your musical knowledge!

If you understand chord construction from the basic triad to all of the chord extensions, you will understand why different chords have a different "feel." And when you are looking to introduce a little different sound to a song you will you will have some ideas about things to try.

If you know the great players of the past and the sound of their music you will be able to introduce some interesting variety in your playing.

Musical knowledge will allow you to communicate with other musicians more effectively. You will be able to share your ideas, and you will more readily learn from others. Musical knowledge helps you become a contributing member of the music community. Participating in online forums is interesting and educational. Lifelong friendships have been formed because of a common interest in music.

Exercise 14.1 Use Knowledge to Improve Your Playing

As your musical knowledge expands, try to apply specific lessons to your playing.

Here are some examples:

If you are using an ear training software package you will be learning to recognize musical intervals and the sound of chord types. Try the following:

1. Fret two notes on the banjo and identify the musical interval between them.
2. Play a basic chord and then alter it somehow (flat the 3rd, add a minor 7th, etc.) and then identify the chord. Also, identify the unique sound you have just created.

As you study great banjo players from the past, you may hear a sound that you really like. This could open up a whole new world of playing - different styles of playing, different techniques - who knows!

As you start to learn about composition and song structure, you might start writing your own songs. If you understand tablature or standard music notation you will be able to save your compositions in written form.

The lesson from nature is that knowledge broadens your perspective and opens up new opportunities. Musical knowledge can make your banjo experience more enjoyable and your playing more interesting.

Chapter 15. Nature's Diversity

Figure 15.1 nature's Diversity

15.1 Nature's Diverse Community

The natural world is filled with diversity and variety. Think how boring things would be if the earth were perfectly smooth with no mountains or valleys, if the wind blew at the same speed all the time, and the temperature was always the same. What would it be like if everything was the same color or all sounds were of the same loudness?

Each animal and plant has a unique set of strengths and abilities that they use to thrive. Some members of nature's community have strength or speed. Some have the ability to blend in with their surroundings. The bear is a powerful animal but he can't glide through the air like a raven in flight. Trees have a variety of bark and leaves. Think about fur, feathers, claws and beaks. What an amazingly diverse community!

Because of this diversity they have different preferences and habits. The same is true for humans. You are a unique individual with unique strengths and preferences that you bring to the banjo.

Activity 15.1 Observe Unique Strengths

On your next trip into the wilderness (or your own back yard) spend some time just looking for and listening to nature's diversity. In fact, use all of your senses: feel the texture of tree bark, smell a leaf, and observe the amazing variety of colors that are all around you.

As you become more familiar with the plants and animals that you are observing, start to understand their behavior. Why do they act the way they do? Most birds love to fly and spend a lot of time in trees, so naturally they build their homes there. Some birds aren't so well suited for flight and spend most of their time on the ground.

Some animals have very keen eyesight or an amazing sense of smell. Some are strong or fast. All of these factors influence their behavior.

In the same way, our unique strengths and interests determine our behavior. Why is one person drawn to bluegrass music and lightning fast breakdowns and another person likes old time music or ballads? Each of us is "suited" to certain banjo styles, and our tastes (and abilities) change over time. There's nothing wrong with that. It's the natural way. Each of us needs to be pleased with our approach to banjo playing.

Exercise 15.1 Decisions Based on Your Unique Strengths

Why do you prefer one style of banjo playing to another? Probably because it "suits" you better. Think about your preferences. Don't be pressured into thinking one way is better than all the others. If you prefer folk music played with a two-finger technique, you have nothing to apologize for. Not everyone likes, or is suited to, playing lightning speed bluegrass breakdowns. Don't let the other guys at the jam session make you feel guilty because you can't play Foggy Mountain Breakdown up to speed. Maybe you will at some point in the future. Maybe you never will! That's OK.

The lesson from nature for me is: maybe I can't soar like an eagle, but I can sing like a songbird.

Also, your preferences can change over time. Several older players have told me how their preferences are much different today from when they were younger.

Take some time to reflect on your preferences and abilities, and enjoy your banjo playing!

Chapter 16. Nature's Jam Session

Figure 16.1 Nature's Jam Session

16.1 Balance, Harmony and Interaction

A jam session can take many forms. They are all fun, but they can be very different. Here are a few types of jam sessions that I have attended:

1. You get together with friends and play songs you already know. It might be a rehearsal for an upcoming gig or just a fun get together to play and swap licks.
2. You attend a song circle and people take turns leading songs they already know. Different people have the opportunity to take a break and play a solo they have already worked out for that song or they just make it up on the spot.

3. You attend a jam and you don't know the songs, but you learn to vamp along with the chord progression.
4. Maybe it's just you and one other person. You choose a key and just jam. It's not really a song anybody knows. It's just a conversation that grows. This type of jam can be the most exciting because you don't know where it will go! You may discover some great new progressions or write a new song.

I think nature's jam session is a conversation. Trees and rocks interact over time. This interaction might not take place in the time frame we are used to, but you can see them interacting.

Birds communicate with each other. Sometimes with mating calls and some times warnings. Maybe sometimes it's just for fun.

Usually the "lead singers" have a backup band consisting of wind, water and trees. If you have ever been to a rock concert you have seen people waving their hands in the air. When you attend Nature's jam session look at the treetops. They are participating in the same way. OK, maybe a little bit over the top, but all of nature sings and we can hear it if we only know how to listen.

16.2 Mountain Music

"Two rushing streams feed the high mountain lake where I sit. Their voices blend as if in song. The wind performs the orchestration by first presenting one melody and then the other. Sometimes they sing together."

I recorded those words on one of my backpacking trips in the Sierra Nevada Mountains of California. I took a rest break by a beautiful mountain lake and started listening to the rushing streams across the valley. It really was musical, and it seemed to me they were "jamming."

16.3 Trees and Rocks

Trees and rocks interact on a different time scale, but they do influence each other.

Figure 16.2 below shows two trees interacting. Notice how they stay out of each other's way just like two players in a jam session. They don't grow branches between them, just on the side facing away from each other.

Figure 16.2 Two Trees Interacting

In Figure 16.3 a tree and a rock are interacting. The rock is not about to move, but the tree says, "I can work around this." If there is a player at a jam session "as stubborn as a rock" you can still work around him and make beautiful music. Who knows, maybe he will get the message.

Figure 16.3 "I can work around this."

The lessons we learn from nature's jam session are:

1. Be sensitive to each other - listen.
2. Complement each other.
3. Stay out of each other's way.
4. Enjoy each other's company.

Activity 16.1 Take Time to Just Listen

This activity might be a little more difficult than the others, but it is important. Go out and listen to nature's jam session. Listen for birds and animals interacting. On a different time scale, look for rocks and trees interacting. Become immersed in nature's interactive community and bring home your insights.

Exercise 16.1 Record Some Interesting Sounds

Another way to bring home the sounds of nature is to record them. You may hear something interesting and want to bring it home to see if you can play along with it. Here are some examples:

1. A waterfall
2. Rain
3. Birdsong
4. The steady tapping of a woodpecker
5. Ocean waves

Exercise 16.2 Let's Jam!

If you attend a regular jam session, think how you might specifically incorporate some of the lessons from nature's jam session. Some ideas to consider are:

1. Listening and interaction
2. Respecting other players
3. Staying out of each others way
4. Complementing the solo

Play along with the field recordings that you have made. Even better, a friend of mine takes his banjo out into his garden and plays quietly. Before long the birds come over and sing with him. Now, that's a jam session with nature!

Chapter 17. Where Do We Go from Here?

Figure 17.1 Where Does the Path Lead?

17.1 The Adventure Continues

We have learned a lot of lessons from nature that can be used to make our banjo playing more enjoyable and as effortless as possible. Also, I hope this book has provided a motivation to enjoy nature at a deeper level. But I think we have only scratched the surface. This is the last chapter of this book, but hopefully only the beginning of the adventure!

I would love to hear about your discoveries! Send me an email at rmckeon5@gmail.com

Also, please visit my website at rickmckeon.com

Meet The Author

Hi, I'm Rick McKeon. I am currently living in beautiful Prescott, Arizona. Since retiring I have been spending time pursuing my passion for writing, playing music and teaching. I am currently producing a series of video lessons on playing the banjo and guitar, and am writing books encouraging people to appreciate nature at a deeper level. I hope some of these ideas have inspired you.

Some of my other pursuits include hiking, backpacking, treasure hunting, exploring old ghost towns and mines, recreational mathematics, photography and experimenting with Microcontrollers.

For more about these activities check my website at rickmckeon.com

Other Books by Rick McKeon

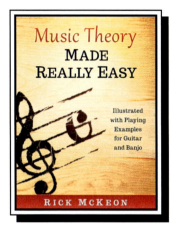

Music Theory Made Really Easy: Illustrated with Playing Examples for Guitar and Banjo
ISBN: 9781544149943

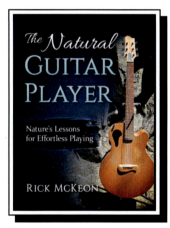

The Natural Guitar Player: Nature's Lessons for Effortless Playing
ISBN: 9781535151924

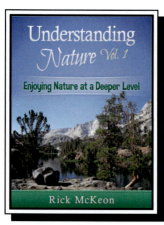

Understanding Nature Vol. 1: Enjoying Nature at a Deeper Level!
ISBN: 9781502510020

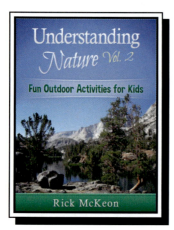

Understanding Nature Vol. 2: Fun Outdoor Activities for Kids
ISBN: 9781515377276

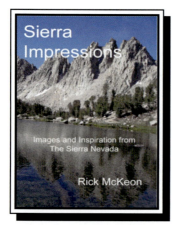

Sierra Impressions: Images and Inspiration from the Sierra Nevada
ISBN: 978131040369

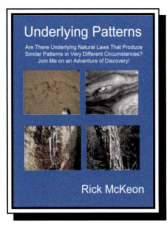
Underlying Patterns: The Search for Patterns in Nature
ISBN: 9781311783615

You Make Us Feel Young Again!
ISBN: 9781310558108

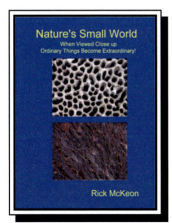
Nature's Small World
ISBN: 9781511965507

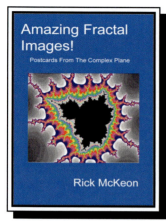

Amazing Fractal Images: Postcards From the Complex Plane
ISBN: 9781311990440

Kailee's Adventures in the Pine Forest: A Young Girl Learns Ancient Secrets from the Trees and Rocks of the Pine Forest
ISBN: 9781514297636

Made in the USA
Monee, IL
22 December 2019